THE PASTOR AS STEWARD

Faithful Manager and Leader

Kenneth H. Carter

DISCIPLESHIP RESOURCES

MATERIALS FOR GROWTH IN CHRISTIAN FAITH AND LIFE

P.O. Box 189 • Nashville, TN 37202 • Phone (615) 340-7284

Library of Congress Card Catalog No. 90-62151

ISBN 0-88177-097-3

DR097B

CONTENTS

For Pam, Elizabeth, and Abby

INTRODUCTION

The heart of the Christian life can be seen in the manner in which people conduct their economic lives and in the way they regard money and possessions. William Barclay noted that a person's character, honesty or dishonesty, straightness or crookedness "can be seen, and nowhere better, than in . . . daily business dealings. The life a [person] lives is in its own way a preparation for eternal life." [1] One's use of and attitude toward "mammon" is indeed central to the teachings of scripture; Jesus spoke more often about the claims, dangers, and proper uses of money and possessions than any other subject, with the exception of the kingdom—a subject certainly not divorced from one's stewardship of time and money.

This centrality of wealth and possessions among God's people has been ignored by some and misunderstood by others. John Wesley acknowledged that "the right use of money (was) a subject largely spoken of, after their manner, by men of the world; but not sufficiently considered by those whom God hath chosen out of the world." [2] Today one notices an abundance of magazines, newsletters, and books offering advice on financial matters, but few take seriously the claims of the Christian faith. Such a vacuum has elicited two responses: cynicism, which sees no relation between business and faith; and a kind of "baptized" version of the American dream, which equates success with faithfulness.

My intention in this brief volume is to suggest an alternative way of envisioning wealth, possessions, and economic practices, particularly among God's people. I offer these reflections in the hope that they will foster dialogue among pastors and intellectually serious laypersons (or perhaps I should say intellectually serious pastors and morally serious laypersons). I also hope this work will serve as a distillation of diverse ingredients that constitute, for me, the crux of the faithful life: how we act as stewards of God's blessings; how we as pastors exercise our stewardship as leaders in the church; and how we translate our creeds, hymns, prayers, and sermons into daily gestures of service to God and neighbor.

Before going further, I should note that this is not a book about *stewardship* as that term is often understood, i.e., as a specialized category or division of the church's program or the individual's witness. The Christian *life* is stewardship, as we are the recipients and representatives of a gracious God who has come to us in Jesus Christ. Thus we will reflect on how we exercise our stewardship as leaders within the church and within our families and marriages, in society and professional life, and as we faithfully engage in action and contemplation.

As a people who live in communion and in common with God, who have offered vows of "time, talents, gifts, and service," and who have taken also the symbol of the stole, it is perhaps mundane to say that all we have and are is due to God's grace and beneficence. As we acknowledge God's claim upon our financial and economic practices, we must struggle with questions of identity, of community, and of vocation. Issues of security, power, and self-worth are shaped by our uses of money. The power of possessions either joins us to or separates us from those who are our brothers and sisters, as well as those called the "least of these" by Jesus. I hope that a recognition of the power of money and possessions will lead us toward creative and faithful stewardship of God's resources and blessings.

My intention is not to engender guilt, or to nourish self-righteousness, or to advocate any particular ideology. I simply wish to identify the powerful role of money and possessions in shaping Christian identity, particularly the identity of the pastor, while wrestling with communal and vocational responses. The difficulty and the importance of such a task seems merited by the attention given to such questions in scripture and in Christian tradition.

I am grateful to the editors of *Books and Religion, Pulpit Digest,* and *Quarterly Review,* in whose pages portions of this work have appeared in slightly different form. Each chapter concludes with a section "For Reflection" and a prayer. The questions and exercises are intended to elicit further reflection and to prompt action; they might also be suitable for use in groups of pastors. The closing prayers place the discussions within the context of our response to God's gracious initiative of creation and blessing and subsequent requirement of faithfulness and servanthood.

I count it a joy and blessing to exercise my pastoral vocation with the members and staff of Christ United Methodist Church. My life has also been enriched by friendships with pastors in my own annual conference and denomination and with those of other traditions. In the spirit of wonder, gratitude, humility, and obligation, I offer these reflections to pastors and to the larger Christian community.

PART ONE:
PERSONAL STYLE

"Manner or method of acting or performing esp. as sanctioned by some standard. a distinctive or characteristic manner."
Webster's New Collegiate Dictionary, 1977

The economic practices of Christians are distinctive because they originate in God's grace and beneficence and have as their end a witness to the world and a service on behalf of the neighbor. The pastor as steward lives out of a constant awareness of this truth.

CHAPTER ONE

WHAT WE DESERVE AND WHAT WE RECEIVE

Ephesians 2

KEY ISSUES

Is life fair? Is God just? How can we as leaders of God's people move men and women to an appreciation of the sheer grace of God and to an acceptance of a grace that is beyond justice or fairness?

Theologian and preacher Karl Barth once observed that "we dislike hearing that we are saved by grace, and by grace alone. We do not appreciate that God does not owe us anything, that we are bound to live from his goodness alone, that we are left with nothing but the great humility, the thankfulness of a child presented with many gifts." [3]

THE PRIMACY OF GRACE

One of the fundamental maxims of Christian belief is that our existence is grounded in the grace of God. We are like children, Barth said, receiving gifts from a loving parent. Another theologian, Stanley Hauerwas, suggests that "to learn to be God's creatures means that we must learn to recognize our existence and the existence of the universe itself as a gift." [4]

Orthodox Christianity has always insisted upon the prevenient grace of God in Jesus Christ for the salvation of the world. This salvation is explicitly spelled out in the Letter to the Ephesians: "By grace you have been saved through faith, and this is not your own doing; it is the gift of God—not the result of works, so that no one may boast" (2:8-9).

Our language, as God's people, is one of grace, of gifts, of givenness. Such language was fundamental to Israel's self-understanding:

2

When the Lord your God has brought you into the land that he swore to your ancestors, to Abraham, to Isaac, and to Jacob, to give you—a land with fine, large cities that you did not build, houses filled with all sorts of goods that you did not fill, hewn cisterns that you did not hew, vineyards and olive groves that you did not plant— and when you have eaten your full, take care that you do not forget the Lord, who brought you out of the land of Egypt, out of the house of slavery (Deut. 6:10-12).

To identify ourselves as God's people is to admit that what we have, what we possess, and what we might lay claim to is in fact a gift, which we in turn accept, rejoice in, and employ for God's purposes and to God's ends. To serve as pastoral leaders is to say, with Wesley, "I am no longer my own, but Thine" (Covenant Service).

Within our culture, however, we hear a competing language, a different message. We hear that the successful person is one who acquires and that the "good life" is one in which we are free from obligations or commitments to others. This language speaks not of grace and gift, but of acquisition; we are not so much recipients as earners, not stewards but consumers. We have come to be known and identified by what we do and what we own. As this language begins to shape our perceptions and motivations, we find that the assumptions of scripture become foreign to us. Soon our vision becomes attuned to the desire for mammon rather than the experience of God through faithful discipleship.

(FOCUS)

How do we evaluate other pastors? By their gifts, by the capacities God has placed within them for service? Or do we identify them by their place of service and its size and prestige? Take a moment to re-read the last two paragraphs.

In the synoptic Gospels (Matthew, Mark, and Luke), we find the story of the rich young man, who asks of Jesus, "What must I do to inherit eternal life?" Jesus summarizes the law, which the man vows to have observed from his youth. "Go, sell what you own, and give the money to the poor, and you will have treasure in heaven," Jesus responds, sensing that this was the one area of the inquirer's life that had not been relinquished to God (Mark 10:21). At this, the scriptures tell us, the rich young man went away sorrowful, for his possessions were numerous.[5]

AN UNLIKELY PROBLEM

The rich young man's problem was simple: His possessions had begun to define the person that he was, and he was powerless to change. To give away all that he had would be to begin a new life, to take on a new identification, and to understand life in an altogether different manner. Unwilling to heed Jesus' call to surrender, the man was unable to receive. His understanding of possessions prohibited him from knowing life as a gift.

We have a problem with gifts. We say that we like to receive them, yet we are somehow uneasy about receiving a gift. A friend of mine told the story of a couple that he and his wife had known, who were from a foreign country. One evening my friend and his wife had invited the friends over for dinner. They had an elaborate meal, sat for a time afterward, enjoyed dessert and coffee, and also enjoyed each other's company. When the time came for the evening to end, the guests looked at each other and said, "It's time that we headed home," and they left.

Do you notice something missing in the story? If we had been the guests, we would have wanted to say how thankful we were to have been invited, how delicious the food had tasted, and how gracious the hospitality had been.

The friends from a foreign country had a point, though. They knew something about gifts and graciousness that we sometimes forget. They knew that a gift has one purpose: to be enjoyed. Gifts make us uncomfortable because we've forgotten that they are to be enjoyed, to be cherished.

The Bible tells us that our life is a gift. In the beginning God created the heavens and the earth. Life began with God who spoke the earth into being. The Bible tells us that faith is a gift. To trust in God is to come into a relationship that is possible only through God's grace, and not through our intellectual efforts. The Bible tells us that salvation is a gift. We cannot earn God's favor. Salvation is a gift—given to us—or we don't have it at all.

We're not too comfortable with this understanding of life, of faith, and of salvation. Ernest Campbell helped me see this when he noted once that the parable of the laborers in the vineyard has always been the least favorite parable among Christians.[6] You have heard the story in Matthew 20:1-16. Some laborers came to work at 8:00 in the morning and went out into the hot fields. Others came at noon. Off they went to work as well. Finally, at 4:00, the foreman finds two more laborers and asks, "Why aren't you working?" "Because no one has hired us," they reply. They too are hired and go out to work. When five o'clock comes along and everyone knocks off, each worker gets the same pay. The point of the parable is not that we earn what we get, but that God can choose whatever God wants to pay us. Whatever we receive is God's to give. It is all God's gift.

AN EVEN MORE UNLIKELY SOLUTION

When God spoke to Israel of entering into the land of promise, God was speaking to them of grace—of a change in their lives that God would bring about. This change would come through the sheer force of divine power and love. When Paul was summarizing the Christian faith, he used the word *grace.* We can never earn our way into the kingdom of God. Yet, when we come into that relationship, we want to do good works. We love others and we want them to know the richness of our own experience. But we don't do these works to prove ourselves. We are not under the law, but under grace.

Preachers, of which I am one, can be among the most ungracious of folks. I heard the story of two pastors who were in line at a cafeteria. One realized, when he got to the front of the line, that he had no money in his wallet. The other pastor quickly realized what was happening and said to his friend, "I'll loan you the money." "That's mighty gracious of you," the other preacher replied. "Oh no," said the fellow who had helped him out, "it's not grace; I expect you to pay me back!"

We know from reading the scriptures and from experience that our experience of God has been of a different kind. Christians are born, nourished, and sustained by the grace of God. We speak of receiving: "To you it has been given to know the secrets of the kingdom" (Matt. 13:11). We have experienced the mercy of God: "Forgive us our debts, as we also have forgiven our debtors" (Matt. 6:12). With the elder brother of the prodigal son parable we are assured of our inheritance: "Son, you are always with me, and all that is mine is yours" (Luke 15:31). And we rejoice not in the wages that we have earned before God but in the free gift (Romans 6:23).

An understanding of life and existence as gift is essential if we are to live together as God's people. There is a linguistic commonality between the word *grace (charis)* and the word *gratitude (eucharistia)* that indicates how life in Christ is to be lived. Geoffrey Wainwright has suggested that "in worship we receive the self-giving love of God, and the test of our thankfulness is whether we reproduce that pattern of self-giving in our daily relationships with other people."[7] As we have been graced and gifted by God, our lives are permeated with gratitude. Because we have received the grace of God, we are equipped to lead others into lives of grace.

Entry into the promised land is an experience of grace, of hospitality, of security, and of provision, all of which come from the power and mercy of God. Such an experience should lead us toward a continual affirmation of God's graciousness and to the confession that our graciousness to others is given—not because they deserve, for neither do we—but because we are imitators of the One who is rich in mercy. To live by faith is to acknowledge that we live in houses that we do not build and eat the fruit of vines that we do not plant. When we have eaten and are full, we are to "take heed lest we forget," says the Lord. There is indeed a great difference between what we deserve and what we have received.

FOR REFLECTION

1. Using a concordance, note passages of scripture in which you find the words *grace, gift,* and *thanksgiving.* Record any new insights into the character of God and human relationships that you receive.
2. Do we recognize our existence as a gift? How can we learn to recognize it as such?
3. Examine your own life, especially persons close to you and key events. Describe some ways in which the goodness in your life has come, not as the result of your labors, but as a "gift."
4. Should the recipients of church mission funds or philanthropy be "deserving" or "worthy"? Why do we have difficulty giving to those who do not merit assistance?

PRAYER

O God,
as a child I learned to say grace at table:
"Thank you, Lord, for this food,
which has come from your hands."
Help me to see all of life as the table
that you have spread before me.
Remind me that all of life is grace,
that existence is a gift.
Let me respond in gratitude,
through Jesus Christ,
your Gift to and for the world. Amen.

CHAPTER TWO

IDOLATRY AND OTHER
TRIVIAL PURSUITS

Exodus 20

> ### KEY ISSUES
>
> Where are we going? How do we discern our goals?
> What is our "bottom line," and how do we measure it?
> Would we recognize idolatry, or something resembling
> it, if it were present in our lives?

The Christian life, according to scripture and tradition, is first of all the orientation of men and women toward God. God alone is worthy of praise. God is worthy of praise because God is our Creator and our Redeemer. Yet the scriptures also teach us that the authenticity and sincerity of our praise is measured by our daily lives. In other words, our relationship to God is bound up with our relationship to the entire created order. There is no separation between worship and life, between Sunday and Monday, between proclamation and shepherding, between the spheres of church and business, between the sacred and the profane. *"Pro-fano"* literally means "outside the temple." By faith we affirm that the God who is One has called all that exists into being.

NO OTHER GODS

God has a claim upon us. We acknowledge this in the article of faith: "I believe in God the Father Almighty, Maker of Heaven and Earth." To worship God and to confess Jesus Christ as Lord is to locate life's center in this relationship. The unhappy experience of men and women has been that we have rejected this claim. We have settled for less. We have been attracted to lesser gods (Romans 1:23-25).

The Apostle Paul described the problem of idolatry as exchanging the glory of the immortal God for the service and worship of the created order. Though our idolatrous practices may not be as obvious as some that Paul encountered, they are just as real and as dangerous to the health and vitality of our lives. If the starting place of the Christian journey is the reality of God's creation, the tragic turn, enacted continuously among God's people, is that we have chosen our own route. We have oriented our lives along a different course.

> **FOCUS**
>
> Why did you enter the ordained ministry in the first place? What did you hope to see happen? What did you hope to accomplish? Have your goals, aspirations, and dreams changed along the way?

The Ten Commandments in the Hebrew scriptures are set within the context of God's saving activity on behalf of Israel. The first commandment is emphatic: "You shall have no other gods [besides] me" (Exodus 20:3). At first glance, this verse of scripture poses little threat to most of us; we have made our commitments to the God and Father of our Lord Jesus Christ. Surely, we are not planning to bow before strange or foreign gods.

But consider the commandment in a different light. What if "gods" are to be understood in a broader context? Thus "gods" are those realities that claim our absolute devotion and commitment, that carry ultimate meaning for us. Reinhold Niebuhr acknowledged that humanity could not be content merely to possess things and to make them; "inevitably," he insisted, "we worship the things that are meant as means. . . . We worship the things that ought to be means, and we make them ends in themselves, indeed we make them God."[8] We have a skewed sense of discrimination; our hierarchy of values is misplaced. As creative persons we are charged with the responsibility of living in freedom, yet we continually subordinate the purposes of God to our own. The result, Niebuhr reminds us, is the "fact of idolatry."

What are these gods in our lives? They are those realities that claim our "time, talents, gifts, and service." How do we employ our time? John Wesley was meticulous in his management of time and in his recording of those matters to which he gave his energies. As pastors we often complain about the lack of time. Many pastors work fifty hours a week and more, yet we often wonder—to ourselves and to anyone who will listen—"Where does the time go?" The Wesleyan example of keeping a log might assist us in the stewardship of our time.

BREAD THAT PERISHES

Jesus Christ is the bread of life. He gives the bread from heaven, which satisfies, which gives "life to the world," in the words of John the Evangelist. After Jesus had fed the 5,000, the crowds continued to follow him. Then Jesus realized what had been happening: The folks were following him merely for food, solely for the physical satisfaction that came from the loaves of bread that had been multiplied out of the little boy's basket. When he looked back to see those coming after him, Jesus said, "Very truly, I tell you, you are looking for me, not because you saw signs, but because you ate your fill of the loaves" (John 6:26). Then Jesus said to those gathered there, and to us, "Do not work for the food that perishes, but for the food that endures for eternal life" (John 6:27).

In a consumer culture, we are easily defined by those material goods that occupy our attentions and energies, such as a certain car and particular types of clothing. Such a fascination with being current and accepted can occur in the spiritual life as well. Alan Jones has observed that "the spiritual supermarket tries to cater to our longings, fantasies, and hopes. It stimulates my appetite, but rarely satisfies my deepest hungers."[9] The alternative, the bread that comes down from heaven and endures to eternal life is the body of Jesus Christ, his "flesh" (John 6:51). We participate in this body through the church, particularly as we hear the word and partake of the eucharist, and as we give ourselves to and for the world. Wise pastors understand that the sustaining realities of this community are word and sacrament; not coincidentally, these two acts are the primary constituent elements in our ordination. For us the word of Jesus is a necessary one as well: "I am the bread of life," Jesus proclaims. Yet we continue to succumb to the temptation to labor for bread that perishes.

An examination of the self will often bring our own priorities to the surface: Where is our time going? For what purposes are our funds being spent? With whom do we spend time outside of work, and why? Are these areas of our lives strengthening our faith and our ministries, and are they manifestations of our belief in the God who is One? Do these pursuits have any lasting significance? Or are we laboring for bread that is perishing?

GIFTS AND SERVICE

How do we employ our talents? Are our abilities and gifts directed toward the strengthening of the body of Christ? I once met a master woodcarver. His beautiful animals had been featured in museums across the country. This quiet man's gift was hindered, however, by a constant bout with alcoholism. Knowing this, I was surprised that he offered to tutor a vacation church school class in woodcarving. Everyone has a gift, a talent to share. With whom we share that gift and how we share it are questions that indicate our loyalties.

We will speak more later of employing our gifts for God's purposes. Suffice it here to say that we tend to spend money on those matters that we sense to be most important. Some families place a priority on education, and great efforts are expended toward that end; others long for a family "getaway," a vacation home or cabin; others place great importance on clothing, travel, recreation, and various other interests. Our financial resources have a way of flowing to those matters that are meaningful to us.

A popular song of years ago was crafted around the refrain, "You gotta serve somebody." By our very nature we are men and women who focus our lives around some force or direction, whether good or evil; some speak of positive and negative addictions. To give our service to God is to make our lives count for the upbuilding of the kingdom, to work for the increase of the love of God and neighbor.[10]

Most of us quickly realize that there are numerous contenders for the position that God alone demands in our lives. Yet the scriptures are clear: "He is a jealous God"; "The Lord our God is one Lord." That we settle for less, that we engage in trivial pursuits is a sign of our human limitation and failure. The good news is that the One who demands our all—our time and talents, our gifts and service, our energies and abilities—is also the One who is worthy of our ultimate loyalty. As Augustine's prayer has it, "Thou hast made us for Thyself, and our hearts are restless until they find their rest in Thee."[11]

FOR REFLECTION

1. What subtle idolatries have crept into your life?
2. Locate the word *idolatry* in the dictionary. Then note several references to "idols" in scripture, giving special attention to passages in Isaiah and Ezekiel. What new insights have you gained?
3. What doubts, fears, and anxieties keep you from total and unconditional loyalty to God?
4. Commit the famous Augustine affirmation to memory: "Thou hast made us for Thyself, and our hearts are restless until they find their rest in Thee." Recall the words of Jesus: "Where your treasure is, there will your heart be also."

PRAYER

O God,
truly life does not consist in the abundance of things,
but in the knowledge of You.
Where we have fashioned competing gods,
remind us, in your mercy,
that you alone are the Lord.
May our hopes, dreams, and ambitions
be directed toward the fulfillment of your promises
and to the manifestation of your glory,
through Jesus Christ,
the image of the invisible God,
in whom and for whom
all things were created. Amen.

CHAPTER THREE

BLESSED ARE THE POOR?

Matthew 5

KEY ISSUES

How can we know the presence of God amidst the
variety of claims upon our lives? How can we find
blessing in relinquishing that which is an obstacle to
the life of grace? How do we model such a form of
leadership in the community of faith?

In an eloquent prayer of intercession, Ernest Campbell identified the
plight of many when he remembered "those who have so much
wealth that they prize possessions more than people, and worry
into the night about losing what they have." [12] We are a wealthy nation,
by the standards of the world. However, if we take the Beatitudes of
Jesus seriously, we realize that we are not a blessed nation. In the
Beatitudes we hear the saying, "Blessed are you who are poor, for
yours is the kingdom of God" (Luke 6:20). Instead of an announce-
ment of blessing, we are more likely to be in need of a different word
from Jesus: "Do not worry about your life, what you shall eat, or about
your body, what you will wear" (Luke 12:22), or "Do not store up for
yourselves treasures on earth, where moth and rust consume and
where thieves break in and steal" (Matthew 6:19).

ANXIETY AND FREEDOM

The recognition of a relation between anxiety and wealth is an
important undercurrent in the liberation theologians' proclamation to
North American Christians. Significantly, many are beginning to note
the particular relevance of this underdeveloped theme for those strug-
gling to be faithful to Christian values while also living in a culture
whose ethos is often at odds with those teachings and where, as

someone has noted, consumption is the "dominant sporting event" in American life.

In his perceptive analysis of the place of Catholicism in American life, John Coleman insists that Christians are called to a "theology of relinquishment" as a just response to those in need and as a means to interior freedom. Philip Turner, an Anglican moral theologian, interprets the Matthean "spiritualization" of the Beatitude (the poor "in spirit" are blessed) as a recognition of the interior freedom that comes when one is dependent upon God. Turner admits that this has not been a dominant theme in recent liberation theology for good reason: Such an emphasis could be employed as justification for accepting poverty, hunger, and injustice. Yet he suggests that it is nonetheless true: To relinquish one's goods is to embark on the path that leads to freedom in Christ.[13]

GRACE IN LETTING GO

Biblical warrant for the practice of relinquishment can be expressed in a negative form, such as the danger of possessions. The scriptures also continually place emphasis upon relinquishment as a positive way of Christian living. This is evident, for example, in the practice of the apostles who, after extending the right hand of fellowship to Paul, entrusted him with the preaching mission to the Gentiles and then admonished him to "remember the poor." Reflecting on this charge, Paul acknowledged that such a task was "actually what I was eager to do" (Gal. 2:10).

FOCUS

How do we "remember the poor" in our daily ministries? How do our congregations make the poor an integral part of their planning and mission?

In his letter to the Philippians, Paul gives thanks for a gift which the church had forwarded to him. A partnership had been formed between Paul and the Philippians, a bond created by giving and receiving on both sides. This bond is often experienced by those who engage in some form of Christian service, no matter how small—whether it be dishing up soup in a food center or taking Christmas gifts to disadvantaged children. One experiences the grace of God perhaps most powerfully in the act of giving. Of course the opposite is also true: Some people have never been able to give freely and joyfully of time or talents, and their Christian lives are limited by a kind of destructive spiritual poverty.

A moving illustration of a very different kind of attitude toward life was recounted by John Killinger in describing the experience of leaving Vanderbilt Divinity School to assume the pastorate of First Presbyterian Church in Lynchburg, Virginia:

> While I was cleaning out the files in my office, my colleague in the next office was also preparing to leave. He was a Jewish rabbi, and he had been at the university much longer than I. In fact, Lou was retiring. He and his wife, Helen, had looked forward to retirement for years. They loved to travel and planned to spend six months a year in the states and six months in Europe. But a year before Lou's retirement, Helen developed cancer. She died last fall. I stood at his door and watched him shuffle about among the packing boxes and books. It was so sad. Helen had been his inspiration. She had been his organizer, his prompter, his care-taker. His whole future had collapsed when she died. And now he was moving—out of their house, out of his office, out of his old life. "Lou," I said, "I don't know how you do it." "There is a line I keep saying to myself," he said. "It's from 'Der Rosenkavalier.' 'One must be light; with light heart and light hands, hold and possess, hold and let go.'"[14]

To envision life not as possession but as gift, not to be grasped but to be cherished—this is the beginning of graced living. The contempla-tives have understood this very simple point; relinquishment moves us toward an experience of the grace of God, of which we become recipients and instruments. In his classic *Beginning to Pray,* Anthony Bloom notes:

> It is only those who give everything away who become aware of true, total, final, irremediable, spiritual poverty, and who pos-sess the love of God expressed in all His gifts. One of our theolo-gians has said "All the food in the world is divine love made edible." I think this is true and the moment we try to be rich by keeping something safely in our hands, we are the losers, because as long as we have nothing in our hands, we can take, leave, do whatever we want. This is the Kingdom, the sense that we are free

from possessions, and this freedom establishes us in a relationship where everything is love—human love and divine love.[15]

A SENSE OF WHO WE ARE

A final element in the Christian's examination of relinquishment must be the question of identity. After all, we call ourselves "Christians," after the One who "emptied himself, taking the form of a slave. . . . And being found in human form, he humbled himself and became obedient to the point of death—even death on a cross" (Philippians 2:7-8). One cannot deny the dominant emphasis throughout the New Testament upon the self-giving of Jesus; Jesus comes not to be served but to serve (Mark 10:10). He washes the disciples' feet (John 13:1-20). Ultimately, he offers himself to be crucified (Matthew 27).

An identification with Jesus must necessarily run counter to the cultural drive toward consumption and the abundance of possessions. We purchase clothing, automobiles, and food so that we will consciously or subconsciously identify with those who are like-minded. The symbols on our shirts, automobiles, and tennis shoes bear the same message: I am a certain type of person.

All of this becomes problematic for the Christian when we remember that our chief identifying characteristic is to be love. We are known by the mark of Christ that has been imprinted on us and upon our lives as we have died and risen with Christ in baptism and have taken on the towel in servanthood. Our identity is tied to his. To be a Christian implies that our motivations, desires, dreams, and hopes have been shaped by the person of Jesus Christ. To be a representative of the Christian community is to model the self-giving of God. To be Christlike is to journey in a very specific direction: toward love, sacrifice, and service.

Such an approach to living is truly countercultural. Elaine Pagels, in *Adam, Eve and the Serpent,* describes the subversive power of the early Christian proclamation of a humanity created in the image of God and therefore free from tyranny. This interior freedom, grounded in the creation narratives, gave to the early church an identity apart from their relation to the various gods of the empire.[16]

The coexistence of anxiety and wealth points us toward the necessity of interior freedom, shaped by our relation to Christ and rooted in our creation as God's people. As we affirm the words of Jesus, "blessed are the poor," we are challenged to find our identity and security in an unseen reality. Yet therein lie both the risk and the reward of the Christian life.

FOR REFLECTION

1. Have you ever done without something as a spiritual discipline or in order to help someone else? What did you gain from that experience?
2. "Doing without" does not necessarily lead to spiritual growth. For many, material limitation is a hindrance to faith and trust in God. How does such a reality bring our more affluent lifestyles into judgment?
3. Does an abundance of possessions actually simplify our lives? Do these possessions give us more time for those aspects of life that are most important?

PRAYER

O God,
I am preoccupied with things, gadgets.
My life is spent following schedules, attending meetings, meeting deadlines.
I have lost touch with the truth that you are most important.
Help me put aside those things that are peripheral and cling to that which is eternal, life-changing.
Remind me that people are more important than things.
Give me a hunger and a thirst for righteousness, that I might truly be filled.
Through Jesus Christ,
who had no place to lay his head,
and who was finally able to say,
   "Father, into your hands I commend my spirit." Amen.

PART TWO:
FUNDAMENTAL RELATIONS

How we use our time, how we regard our
relations to others, how we envision our place in
the world: In God's economy these are issues of
fundamental importance. Our deliberations in
these areas lead us to the heart of what it is to
be faithful pastors and stewards.

CHAPTER FOUR

Action, Contemplation, and Living in Between: A Meditation on Christian Living

Luke 10

```
┌─────────────( KEY ISSUES )─────────────┐
│                                          │
│  How do we respond to the call to be contemplative
│  servants and scholars? How can we give integrity to
│  the sanctuary and study while also identifying with
│  those in the marketplace? How can we be stewards of
│  time and energy as we serve others?
│                                          │
└──────────────────────────────────────────┘
```

W e are saved by grace; we shall be judged by our works. Go ye into all the world; come apart to a lonely place. Give a cup of cold water; pray without ceasing. As we listen for the call, what are we likely to hear? In times of prayer, we are made to feel guilty for abandoning the world in all of its need. In our acts of compassion, we are reminded of the peril of the neglected inner life. It is almost as if there were a double-mindedness built into the design of the spiritual life.

Take the pastoral ministry, for example. In this profession one can do almost nothing. Stories are told about those pastors who lose themselves in their work quite literally—they hide or make themselves scarce during the week. My brother's wife asked me once, quite honestly, "What do you do during the week?" Yet pastoral ministry can also be the opposite: One can work oneself to death; the pastor can serve without ever taking a vacation or a day off; the day can begin early and end late.

In the pastoral ministry are both scoundrels and saints, charlatans and servants. A wise pastor put it this way: "I realized early on that there is a high road and a low road." A preacher's style might be detailed exegesis or the snappy sermon conversation starter. A pastor might be involved in the life of a people or have only a surface level relationship that never moves beyond the perfunctory. The pastoral ministry is an enigma.

At the core of this enigma is the perennial struggle that has engaged God's people from the beginning: How much of what I am involved in is my own doing (personal agency), and how much is a gift from God (grace)? Is the faithful life primarily one of action or contemplation? Is it more important to be or to do? Most of us find ourselves on a middle way, between pride and sloth, between frenetic activity and hushed stillness. Yet at times we find ourselves looking in one direction or the other, feeling inadequate for not devoting enough time and energy to pastoral calling or for spending too little time in the study or for neglecting our families.

THE GOOD SAMARITAN AND THE BLESSED CONTEMPLATIVE

Acknowledging a pastoral dilemma is one thing; seeking some sort of resolution is quite another. The scriptures, on first glance, are not much help. Two of the most familiar stories in the Bible are found in the tenth chapter of Luke's Gospel, side by side. There we find the parable of the good Samaritan and the telling of Jesus' visit to the house of Mary and Martha.

The first story is a celebrated summons to action, a call to faithfulness in life. The priest and the Levite are unable, despite their religious training and standing, to rescue the wounded man who had fallen among thieves. The Samaritan, outside the law and the religious tradition, proves to be a neighbor to the beaten man. "Does your faith work?" we ask those who listen to our sermons. "Does it help that wounded person we encounter along our daily journeys?"

This message is clear enough. In the next passage, Jesus comes to the home of Mary and Martha. Mary sits at his feet to listen, while Martha is "distracted" with the business of providing hospitality. Jesus' judgment is clear: Martha is anxious, troubled about many things. Mary is single-minded in her attention to that which cannot be taken away from her (the contemplation of his teaching).

A MEDIEVAL DETOUR

Thomas Aquinas, in his discussion of the active and contemplative lives, depended heavily upon the story of Mary and Martha in claiming a superiority for the contemplative rather than the active life. For Aquinas, life was judged according to its end, and the greatest end for humanity was the hope of the "Beatific Vision." This greatest end, which Aquinas also described as happiness, was approached by two means—action and contemplation. Or, life has two elements—the active and the contemplative. Within the intellect there is a twofold division that corresponds to the two lives: the contemplative intellect, which has as its end the knowledge of the truth, and the practical intellect, which is related to external action.[17]

In his treatment of contemplation in *Summa Theologica* (Vol. 2, Part 1), Aquinas employs Gregory's definition of the contemplative life: "The contemplative life is to cling with our whole mind to the love of God and our neighbor, and to desire nothing beside our Creator" (179.2). The love of God, on the one hand, and the love of the neighbor, on the other, pose a dilemma for Aquinas. The former is more suited to the contemplative vocation of men and women, while the latter necessarily issues in external activity.

Aquinas' discussion of action and contemplation proceeds along two lines. First, he discusses the relation between the two as they occur in ordinary human life. He is willing to allow for the exigencies of human existence; although he will generally claim that contemplation is more excellent than action, he does allow for exceptions. Thus, "it may happen that one man merits more by the works of the active life than another by the works of the contemplative life" (2.1.182.2). This might be due to the "immoderation" of one's contemplation; however, Aquinas also alludes to the possibility of individual differences among persons: "He that is prone to yield to his passions on account of his impulse to action is simply more apt for the active life by reason of his restless spirit." Others, however, "have the mind naturally pure and restful, so that they are apt for contemplation, and if they were to apply themselves wholly to action, this would be detrimental to them" (2.1.182.4). In commenting on these different aptitudes, Aquinas judges them both to be noble and proper. Action prepares us for contemplation, and contemplation trains us also for "works of the active life."

Aquinas also discusses the relation of action and contemplation within the context of human need. Not only are different persons disposed to different styles of activities, but we must also encounter different circumstances. The "demands of charity" might call us to help the neighbor in need; in this way the active life is preferable to the contemplative life "in a restricted sense and in a particular case" (2.1.182.1). The active life, nevertheless, is one of "bondage," and because of human necessity, we are to engage in good works only as they dispose us to the life of contemplation.

Aquinas goes further in his analysis of the active and contemplative practices to their "generic" or "essential" relationship. Here the contemplative life is superior to the active life. He depends heavily upon the previously noted story of Mary and Martha (Luke 10:38-42); Mary, who sits and listens at the feet of Jesus, personifies the life of contemplation; Martha, who scurries about performing acts of hospitality, exemplifies the active life. Contemplation, Aquinas argues, is more excellent on several grounds: one acts according to one's highest principles (the intellect) and toward the most proper objects (intelligibles); contemplation is more "continuous" and more "delightful" than action; it is more "self-sufficient" and less dependent on externals than action and is done for its own sake and not for some further end (for it is an eternal pursuit).

David Burrell, in *Aquinas: God and Action,* has noted that Aquinas, in his treatment of the relation between action and contemplation, depends more on Gregory and on the scriptures than on Aristotle:

> Aquinas deals with the issue of the active or contemplative life without a hint of the conflict Aristotle feels in the ETHICS. The Greek philosopher obviously prizes the homo politicus, deeming it necessary to realize one's humanity most fully. . . . Aquinas, however, quotes Gregory more than Aristotle, and glosses Luke 10:42 [the account of Mary and Martha] as his central text.[18]

Burrell criticizes Aquinas for an inadequate account of the active life with respect to human needs. Citing Paul's dilemma in the Letter to the Philippians—" . . . my desire is to depart and be with Christ, for that is far better; but to remain in the flesh is more necessary for you." (1:23-24)—Burrell maintains that Aquinas errs in "too neatly resolving the dilemma of the active and the contemplative lives." Burrell suggests that Aquinas "sounds more Greek and less Christian than Aristotle." This is perhaps due to the nature of the concerns of Aristotle and Paul; the former was engaged in the work of the *polis,* while the latter was involved in the development of new Christian communities. In sum, Aquinas was willing to grant a place for the active life, but only as it relates to and enriches the contemplative life.

ACTION, CONTEMPLATION, AND THE DANGERS OF SPECIALIZATION

We might find reasons other than philosophical and scriptural to question Aquinas' evaluation of the active and contemplative lives. Remember that Aquinas was a contemplative, one dedicated to the life of the mind and its quest for the knowledge and apprehension of God. In our age of specialization, we would find Aquinas a place in the seminary or at a retreat center, where he could proceed in the writing of his *Summa,* unhindered by the needs and demands of the market place—the tasks of ordinary men and women. After all, one might ask how much intellect it really takes to organize a church softball team, to participate in the parish bazaar, or even to administer the church school. These rather mundane aspects of the ministry are best left to others. Many are called; few are chosen, we say tacitly. Aquinas would be "above" the parish ministry.

This thought process leads to the dangerous outcome of the age of specialization—the divorce between action and contemplation. Fred Craddock offers a chilling portrayal of an all-too-frequent occurrence.

> When the life of study is confined to "getting up sermons," very likely those sermons are undernourished. They are the sermons of a preacher with the mind of a consumer, not a producer, the mind that looks upon life in and out of books in terms of usefulness for next Sunday. The last day of such a ministry is as the first, having enjoyed no real lasting or cumulative value in terms of the minister's own growth of mind, understanding, or sympathy.[19]

The encouragement of such practices is the result of a kind of unconscious conspiracy on the part of some of the laity, denominational programs and officials, and, unwittingly, the pastor. Many lay people have little insight into the amount of time necessary for the most basic *public* tasks of the pastor, such as preaching, teaching, and counseling. Small provisions of time or space are made for the life of prayer, study, reflection, and introspection; a visit to the nearest parish will usually bear this out.

To suggest that it ought to be otherwise is to swim against the tide. My friend Ralph Wood, a professor at Wake Forest University, gave the charge to the congregation upon the installation of a new pastor. "Do not settle for *Time*-and-*Newsweek* reports on current events," he advised the congregation. "Refuse sermon illustrations drawn entirely from television sitcoms and ACC athletics. Reject every gimmick, and howl at all sentimentality. Cry out, instead, for the transcendent Word of grace." [20] Such a word is possible, he later noted, only when there has been ample regard for the disciplines of study and prayer, reflection, and contemplation, by pastor and parish alike.

FOCUS

How can you create adequate time and space for the contemplative life? How can you lead people in your local church to discover time for reflection and study in their own lives?

Ours is the malaise of split personality. We are either pietist or intellectual, circuit rider or contemplative, activist or scholar. Yet the cure is perhaps seen in those two familiar stories laid side by side in Luke's Gospel. Together they form a whole, or what scripture scholars have called a "chiastic structure." The literary connectedness of the stories about Mary and Martha and the good Samaritan is indicative of the bond between contemplation and action, love for God and neighbor, prayer and service. The pastor must always recognize this unity, while also acknowledging that most days find us somewhere in between. The relation between action and contemplation has puzzled Christians for centuries and will continue to do so until we are found to be in the presence of God, where all our labors will be praise and where our actions and contemplations will be one in the God who is One. In the meantime we live somewhere in between, with St. Paul, Aquinas, Mary, Martha, the lawyer, the man who fell among thieves, and the good Samaritan.

FOR REFLECTION

1. Are you more prone to action or contemplation? As you were growing up, which was more valued by your family? Which is more valued by society?
2. How do you find time and space for contemplation in your own life?
3. Do you find it easy (or difficult) to recognize a connection between prayer and activity, between action and contemplation?
4. Who is your "hero" in the pastoral ministry, and why? What aspects of his or her life do you find appealing? How is the relationship between action and contemplation evident in his or her life?

PRAYER

O God of Mary and Martha,
help us to speak only after we have listened to you;
help us to rest only after we have labored for you;
guide our hands and our hearts in ways that would please you;
open our minds to consider your ways;
and lift our voices to offer you praise,
through Jesus Christ our Lord. Amen.

CHAPTER FIVE

OF MYSTERY, MANNERS, AND MARRIAGE

Genesis 1

KEY ISSUES

How is marriage a matter of stewardship? How do we live in relationships with creativity and commitment? And how do our relationships mirror the primal biblical image of covenant?

A sketch of the current theological and ethical reflection on marriage is truly a task "not to be entered into unadvisedly, but reverently, discreetly, and in the fear of God." Actually, most discussions on the subject of marriage do not have marriage as their exclusive focus. Instead, authors will touch on matters of commitment, partnership, gender roles, and a biblical theology of male-female relationships. At the heart of the discussions, however, lies the question of how relationships, particularly marriage relationships, are to be evaluated in light of Jewish and Christian traditions.

CREATION

A discussion of male and female roles and relationships must necessarily begin with the creation accounts in Genesis 1–3. In *Till the Heart Sings,* Samuel Terrien contests the assumption that woman is the source of human evil, citing her instead as the crown of creation and the divine remedy for human separation and alienation. Diana and David Garland, in *Beyond Companionship: Christians in Marriage,* emphasize the equality of the creative act: " 'So God created man in his own image, in the image of God he created him; male and female he created them' (Genesis 1:27). He created them; he blessed them and gave them dominion (Genesis 1:28); and in Genesis 5:1-2 he also named them. They were created as equals."[21]

27

Terrien, the Garlands, and Lisa Sowle Cahill, drawing upon the work of Phyllis Trible, respond to the troublesome concept of woman as "helpmeet" (Genesis 2:18, KJV), preferring the more accurate terms *partner* (NEB) or even *savior,* as the Hebrew term is employed for God elsewhere in the Hebrew scriptures. Men and women are created in the divine image for partnership with one another; this is the force of the creation accounts. The reality of human sin, portrayed in Genesis 3, has as its result the description but not the prescription of a male-female hierarchy; as Cahill concludes, "supremacy and subordination, as distinct from difference and cooperation, are not part of the original creation but of the condition of sin." [22]

From similar analyses of these biblical texts, the authors diverge into varied directions. Terrien finds in the scriptures a "God-centered humanism," with man and woman together in pilgrimage toward their existential end, the experience of the presence of the Creator. Such an interpretation is a corrective to any justification of male dominion or supremacy, to women's liberation apart from human liberation, and to what he calls "self-sufficient" humanism.

Diana and David Garland are professors of social work and New Testament, respectively, and their perspective is shaped by an attentiveness to the biblical tradition and to recent empirical studies. While citing the hierarchical and egalitarian models as the prevailing patterns of marriage in our society, they call for something more: "partnership marriage." Partners in marriage are concerned not so much with the structure of the relationship (distribution of power, roles, etc.) as with a commitment to the joint task of discovering a vocation and a purpose within the context of God's will.

COMMITMENT AND COVENANT

Another lens through which the marriage relationship can be examined is through an analysis of this partnership or commitment of two couples to one another. Both Lisa Sowle Cahill and Margaret Farley have produced works that are tightly argued, clearly focused examination of the structures of human relationships. Cahill argues that "what constitutes a convincing case about right and wrong from a Christian point of view," must, "at the level of application," take into account "empirical studies . . . about human sexual experience and gender identity; the ways Christian authors and churches have traditionally educated their faithful to perceive male and female relations, sexuality, and sex; what the Bible says or indicates about these subjects; and even philosophical presentations about them."[23] Cahill's analysis, then, depends upon much more than scripture alone; she also draws from sources ancient and modern, theological and philosophical. These sources have a "dialectical, circular, and critical" relationship to one another within the moral discourse of the Christian community.[24] Cahill concludes that the two criteria that have been and should continue to be normative for sexuality among Christians are committed partnership and procreation; however, she does recognize that there might be morally permissible expressions of sexuality which are located outside of these categories.

The question of commitment is fundamental to human existence; thus argues Margaret Farley in *Personal Commitments,* an examination of our understandings and experiences of commitment. Why do we desire commitments? How is commitment related to freedom and free choice? What are the conditions by which commitments are sustained? How may the obligations to commitment be released? These questions are placed within the context of the covenant tradition in biblical literature. God's promises and commitments to Israel and to the church have the potential to guide, instruct, and transform our human commitments.

The metaphor of covenant is also central to the thesis of Ray Anderson and Dennis Guernsey, who see the "basic structure of the quintessential order of the family as [being] grounded in God's covenant love, experienced in good parenting, expressed through marriage, and culminating in spiritual maturity and the freedom of fellowship and participation in the church as the new family of God."[25] While Anderson and Guernsey represent a more evangelical theological perspective than either Cahill or Farley, their use of biblical materials and categories (election, adoption, covenant) presents a coherent and refreshing theological paradigm in evaluations of family relationships.

In the diverse methodologies and perspectives represented by the works under consideration, there are common motifs: mutuality and partnership, creation and covenant, commitment and community. Terrien's argument is more aesthetic. Cahill and Farley are more analytical. The Garlands, Anderson, and Guernsey reflect a more pastoral orientation. Yet each avoids the sentimentality and individualistic biases that characterize so much of the reflection on marriage and sexuality.

Cahill's insistence upon the Christian community's role in the evaluation of sexual practices and the Garlands' affirmation of marriage as vocation are positions that I hope will gain ascendency over the prevailing understandings in theological and social-scientific literature. Both of these emphases ought to resonate with the experience of pastors. Pastors regularly observe the impact of marital change upon a local congregation, and we also happily experience the witness of those who see their marriages and homes as contexts for faithful discipleship and service. This is also stressed in the intercessory prayer found in the "Service of Christian Marriage":

> Enable them to grow in love and peace
> with you and with one another all their days,
> that they may reach out
> in concern and service to the world;
> through Jesus Christ our Lord.[26]

Taken together, these moral and theological engagements with issues of relationship, sexuality, and marriage are marked by an intellectual seriousness that is welcome indeed, and which will hopefully shape the ways we have understood this dimension of the Christian pilgrimage.

One's marriage relationship is indeed a "school for character," in the words of Martin Luther, and a potential vehicle for discipleship. That the church has allowed the perspectives of other disciplines (as valid as they might be) to take precedence over serious theological reflection is illustrative of our accommodation to cultural values. A recovery of the theological tradition will also assist the pastor in defining his or her own role in the marriages of parishioners. This recovery might fill the vacuum that cries out for a modern-day Dietrich Bonhoeffer, whose "Wedding Sermon from a Prison Cell" is a model of theologically informed pastoral guidance, or of the sustained reflection of a Karl Barth on matters of sexuality, marriage, and parenting.[27] Amidst warnings about a disintegration of the institutions of marriage and family, the pastor would do well to draw upon the rich heritage of faith in guiding men and women in marriage.

FOR REFLECTION

1. What good reasons can you give for getting married? For staying single?
2. How has the marriage covenant been a part of your own experience of marriage?
3. How might marriage and stewardship be related? How might a couple best work out issues of time, money, energy, and goals in light of a shared commitment and covenant?

PRAYER

O God,
let us always be aware of your presence in marriage;
let us always avail ourselves of your strength
as we live together in marriage;
let us always look to your will
as we seek to be faithful servants in marriage.
Through Jesus Christ our Lord. Amen.

CHAPTER SIX

THE SPIRE AND THE MARKETPLACE

Matthew 25

```
┌─────────────── KEY ISSUES ───────────────┐
```

As pastors, should we get "involved" with money? Are we not called to a nobler, more spiritual vocation? Or do we exercise our callings in the midst of a world of economic realities and loyalties, a world in which Jesus served and to which he spoke with compassion and candor?

U pon leaving the first session of a graduate seminar, I asked the fellow who had sat beside me about his college studies. "I majored in both religion and economics," he replied, "so I suppose I'm qualified to begin my own cult." The intended humor in his response was an indication of the uneasy relation between spiritual faith and material possessions, religion and economy, God and mammon.

When I was ordained, the bishop read the traditional Wesleyan question, "Are you in debt so as to embarrass your ministry?" He then recounted one pastor's response: "No, I've been in debt so long that I'm not embarrassed anymore."

Money can be a problem not only in the personal life of the pastor, but in her or his work as well. How one is doing in a particular field of labor is often gauged by the financial giving of the flock. Money has a curious and sometimes troubling relationship to the work of the pastor and the church: On the one hand, we recognize that ministries need funding, that we are to be stewards of God's blessings. On the other, we are often inclined to view the world of business and money as a strange and foreign land, where the gospel seems alien and out of place.

What is the response of the church to the powerful claims made by money and the world of business? James Gustafson has observed that "some conditions have to be developed before churches can become communities of moral discourse, not the least being better recruitment and training of clergy." This position is based on the contention that most persons of professional effectiveness find little assistance from their churches in thinking about professional responsibilities. Churches use professional persons—a banker, for instance, to handle parish finances—for their own institutional purposes; within limits this is correct. But do churches provide the intelligent leadership or the occasions for professional persons to become more morally effective, to see their ways through moral dilemmas in their own work, to see possibilities in the improvement of society? [28]

The churches' responses to the dilemma have been as varied as our respective theological underpinnings. Some note a great schism between faith and the marketplace. Here the line of separation can be drawn in either "other-worldly" or "this-worldly" terms. Thus we sing:

> On Jordan's stormy banks I stand,
>   and cast a wishful eye;
> to Canaan's fair and happy land,
>   where my possessions lie. [29]

Or we ask the question, unfairly ridiculed by Michael Novak, "Can a Christian be a capitalist?" There has indeed been a strong emphasis in the Christian tradition, perhaps most explicitly stated in the "Social Encyclicals of Catholicism," on the communitarian character of just economic practices.

At the other end of the spectrum, many have insisted on a kind of "gospel of wealth." This position, which can range from the sincere to the absurd, has a long and checkered tradition in North American Christianity. Scriptural justification for those is found in the parable of the talents (Matthew 25:14-30), where Jesus rewards those who multiply what they have been given. Curiously, the parable is set alongside the account of the Great Judgment (Matthew 25:31-46), a passage that contradicts the notion of personal wealth as the goal of life. The rewarded, in this case, are those who feed the hungry, clothe the naked, visit the imprisoned, and so on.

These two passages, the parable of the talents and the account of the Great Judgment, have achieved privileged positions among people of faith who are worlds apart in their understanding of Christian responsibility and obligation. Thus one can ground a business ethic in a call for social justice, or in a recognition of human creativity, or in the doctrine of original sin. Each is valid; each is a part of the tradition; each has its place. Together they contribute to the confusion and diversity of thought that is evident in the church.

FOCUS

After reading these two biblical passages (Matthew 25:14-46), explore underlying connections that might be present in their relationship to one another. How can we develop practices as pastoral leaders that incorporate truths found in each passage?

How can the churches offer the kind of leadership alluded to by James Gustafson? How can the churches provide the contexts for evaluation of economic practices in light of Christian faith? Both Gustafson and Donald Jones have encouraged clergy to educate themselves in the moral and ethical issues surrounding economic practices. The absence of such training in seminaries and divinity schools, according to Jones, is the result of the ascendancy of particular theological perspectives. Social gospel advocates and liberation theologians have called for a "fundamental restructuring" of economic life in modern society, while Christian "realists," such as Reinhold Niebuhr, have judged political ethics (with particular interests in matters of war and peace and race relations) to be more important and urgent than business and professional practices. Thus, business ethics as a discipline is dismissed as either counterproductive (to the cause of economic revolution) or parochial (in light of more pressing matters).[30]

In addition, the churches must recognize that mission and witness are often influenced and shaped by prevailing economic forces. Liston Pope's *Millhands and Preachers* and the sequel, *Spindles and Spires,* by Earle, Knudsen, and Shriver, are excellent descriptions of how religious life has been shaped by economic culture in one particular city (Gastonia, North Carolina). There is no sacred history that exists alongside or above economic, political, and social factors. The claims of God and mammon are woven together, and while the task of sorting them is difficult, it is also a necessary one.

Finally, churches are called to embody an alternative economic vision. The Anglican moral theologian Philip Turner suggests that as the churches ignore or postpone the question of how "the distribution and disposal of money within the church is to be ordered," they "jettison the real chance they have, through the witness of their common lives, to exert moral influence in the system."[31] Stanley Hauerwas' contention that the church *is* a social ethic echoes this same sentiment: We do not stand apart from economic systems, our hands clean and our minds on loftier matters; instead, we engage in political and economic tasks as we do ministry together.

The ethical and moral implications of business and economic practices should be of urgent concern for those within the Christian community. Questions of vocation, stewardship, economic justice, and professional standards challenge us not only as citizens but as people of faith. In a culture that is prone to secluding the claims of faith from the "realities" of the marketplace, a recognition by the church of their necessary interconnectedness might be a good starting place.

FOR REFLECTION

1. How has the church had an effective witness to North America's economic life?
2. What should be the church's own economic witness? How does your own local parish employ its own economic resources?
3. How could pastors and church leaders become more knowledgeable about business and economic practices?

PRAYER

God of spire and marketplace,
whose presence is always in our midst,
comforting, correcting, challenging:
Give us a creativity born of your Spirit;
Give us a compassion formed by the mind of Christ.
Where our economic practices would ignore
the claims of faith;
where our spiritual life is devoid of concern
for the world of flesh and blood:
Guide us in your paths,
strengthen us in your peace,
embrace us in your mercy.
Through Jesus Christ our Lord. Amen.

PART THREE:
VOCATIONAL TASKS

To work, to rest, to prophesy—these are the
elements of a delicate balance that defines our
lives as leaders of God's people. In isolation each
can lead to a skewed sense of purpose, but they
can work together to allow us to be of service,
to be personally sustained, to give and to receive,
and to exercise our vocations as pastors and
stewards.

CHAPTER SEVEN

Of Human Toil, Daily Bread, and Common Life

Genesis 1:26-27

> **KEY ISSUES**
>
> Do we live to work, or do we work to live? Or, phrased differently, do our labors define us as human beings, created in the image of God, or are they simply what we do to put food on the table and keep the bill collectors at bay? How does the pastor lead others toward an appropriate estimate of the value and purpose of work?

The question of work—its meaning and purpose and its rewards and punishments—continues to prompt reflection from theologians, social scientists, economists, and ethicists. The Christian tradition has contended that work has a divine character to it. This idea is expressed in the saying *laborare est orare,* to work is to pray. Robert Calhoun described the response of the person to God as "the antiphony of worship and work." For the person of faith, one's labors serve as a means of drawing one into communion with God. The Christian doctrine of creation is bound to the vocation of men and women who have been created in the divine image. This vocation is portrayed simply enough in the scriptures:

> Then God said, "Let us make humankind in our image, according to our likeness; and let them have dominion over the fish of the sea, and over the birds of the air, and over the cattle, and over all the wild animals of the earth." So God created humankind in his image, in the image of God he created them; male and female he created them. God blessed them, and God said to them, "Be fruitful and multiply, and fill the earth and subdue it; and have

dominion over the fish of the sea and over the birds of the air and over every living thing that moves upon the earth (Genesis 1:26-28).

WORK AND MEANING

In *Modern Work and Human Meaning,* John C. Raines and Donna C. Day-Lower have insisted that to be human is to work. We do not merely work in order to live—we live in order to work. Through work we "express our human essence . . . [as] a species that lives by way of a skill"[32] and we discover our identities within communities of fellow workers. Thus human work has the capacity to assist us on the journey toward "human being and human becoming," or, conversely, "to bring about personal humiliation and dehumanization." The absence of work is necessarily joined to the experience of alienation from community. Others, most notably Philip Wogaman, author of *Economics and Ethics: A Christian Inquiry,* have seen work as an important aspect of human and social fulfillment.

Raines and Day-Lower's study is set within the context of the declining economic realities of the northeastern United States, particularly the steel industry of Pittsburgh. The personal narratives of displaced workers speak of the loss of self-worth, the disintegration of family and social life, and a kind of bereavement over the death of the American dream. The purposes of the Creator God are thus contrasted with the realities of the marketplace, the factory, and the unemployment line. The order, harmony, and bliss of the creation is now engulfed by chaos, alienation, and estrangement.

(FOCUS)

Recall an experience of pastoral care offered to a person undergoing a work-related crisis. How do our identities become shaped by and attached to our work? How can we offer ministry to those whose identities must be rebuilt in the light of work-related crises?

How is this contrast to be resolved? Between the possibilities and the actualities of human work? Between what is and what might be? One resolution, which has much to commend itself in the Jewish and

Christian traditions, is to support a more limited and realistic understanding of the purpose of work. Thus, as Gilbert Meilaender suggests, we do not so much "live to work," in the sense that work brings fulfillment and pleasure to life, as we "work in order to live."

> When the system of vocations as we experience it today is described in terms which make the work the locus of self-fulfillment, Christian ethics ought to object—on the empirical grounds that this is far from true, and on the theological ground that vocation ought not make self-fulfillment central. [33]

Can we experience work as a process of "co-creation" with God? Possibly, but the experience of most is surely different. Studs Terkel begins his introduction to *Working* with these candid words: "This book, being about work, is, by its very nature, about violence—to the spirit as well as to the body." [34] David Halberstam movingly describes the impressions of a journeyman diemaker's first day at a new shop:

> On Monday Goddard bought new work clothes. On Tuesday he went to work. The first thing he noticed that morning was the icy stares of the workers as he walked from one end of the plant to the other. There was no energy, no life, in that cold and hostile place. As Goddard later put it, they were men whose bodies were alive but whose minds and souls had died. [35]

Any occupation or vocation, of course, carries with it the possible outcome of death of mind and spirit. There are those in sales whose hearts are no longer in it, teachers who long ago gave up the life of the mind, and pastors who coast from one parish to the next. If there seems to be abundant evidence against the idea that work is always a means of self-fulfillment, there is present also a variety of coping mechanisms. For example, many find meaning in other realms of life, such as in community, within the family, in voluntary associations, and in friendships.

Both Raines and Day-Lower envision work as an intrinsically human activity, and each insists on some kind of "human right" to work. To speak of rights in any meaningful sense is also to speak of another's duty. For example, if I as a pastor have a "right" to a pastoral appointment, then some system, such as an annual conference, must exist that has a "duty" to supply the appointment.

On this point, Philip Wogaman is more forthcoming than many others. He develops specific criteria for governmental jobs. Among his criteria are the ideas that the jobs should be useful to society; they should require discipline; they should be as interesting as possible; and they should be at or near the minimum wage.[36] Such a program seems ambitious, and it also goes against the political grain of the past decade; yet honest evaluation of our jobs is necessary if we truly believe that the work we do is central to an understanding of ourselves as men and women in partnership with the God who creates. The tension between work as it is and work as it might be mirrors a society in which some people labor in creative ways while others experience alienation and dehumanization.

CHRIST AND COMMUNITY

A creative response to questions of how we use the rewards from our labors can be seen in John Haughey's *The Holy Use of Money*. Haughey, a Jesuit priest, puts forth an imaginative analysis of existing economic practices and how these practices might be transformed or "sublated" by Christ. Just as Philip Turner's *Sex, Money and Power* was a serious attempt to understand economic life from a communal perspective, *The Holy Use of Money* is grounded in Christ's life, teaching, and intentions for human society.

Haughey's thesis is that Christ's relationship to our economic life is one of "sublation": A "given economic system would be sustained and transformed by Christ without its being ignored, loathed, overrun or tolerated by him."[37] The use of the term *sublation,* a word taken from the Christological discussions of the early church, is intentional, as redemption occurs not only because of Jesus' divinity but also through his humanity. Such a process of humanization is at the very core of the Christian's calling as a participant in economic life. Obedience to Christ will necessarily issue in reverence for the world, as it has been transformed by and made a part of Christ. Just as Jesus, according to Christian tradition, is fully human and fully divine, the faithful Christian community, as the Body of Christ, will necessarily enter fully into the life of the world, including the economic sphere.

(**FOCUS**)

How can we bring humanity into our education and efforts in the area of local church stewardship? How can we erase the gap between the human and the divine as we seek to fund the mission and ministry of Christ's church in the world?

Most would agree that the role of community is essential in evaluating economic practices. The community is often where identity and purpose are discovered, so when a factory closes, a way of life ends. Ideally, one's work or calling *(kaleo)* contributes to the community *(ecclesia)*. A communal critique of economic practice recognizes the interrelatedness of rich and poor, advantaged and disadvantaged. Thus the "preferential option for the poor" expresses both the community's greatest need and the means of "healing the entire social body." [38]

Varied discussions of economic life are helpful in depicting the often tenuous relationship between how we ought to earn, spend, and distribute our money, and how we as a society actually carry out those activities. Pastors and leaders in churches carry a great burden in modeling and articulating a faithful and creative relationship among work, faith, and community. The approaches of Haughey and Turner, a Jesuit and an Anglican, respectively, seem to be both innovative and traditional in noting the importance of Christology and ecclesiology in these discussions. The lack of a clear, decisive prescription for engaging faithfully in work and in economic matters, however, might best be attributed to the complexity of the relationship among our labors, our rewards, and our life in common.

FOR REFLECTION

1. Does your own work draw you into communion with God? Do you think it could do so?
2. Is your identity defined by your work? Think about your life without that work. Consider being in a different work setting.
3. Does business have an obligation to serve the common good? Why or why not?

PRAYER

(Begin with prayers of intercession for those without work and for those who must make decisions about the work of others.)

O God of Creation,
you call us to have dominion,
to labor in your vineyards,
to serve you and one another.
Lead us to discover ways of faithfulness
in life and in labor;
teach us to listen for the antiphony of work and worship;
and draw us together in one Spirit
to a common experience of the
presence of Jesus Christ your Son,
in whose name we offer these prayers. Amen.

CHAPTER EIGHT

CATCHING OUR BREATH

Genesis 2

> ### KEY ISSUES
>
> How do we experience renewal and recreation as pastors? How can we incorporate Sabbath observance into our witnesses and into our leadership styles? How can Sabbath observance become an act of faith and trust for the pastor and congregation?

Creation is not an issue that divides the Christian family, but a mystery before which we stand in awe and reverence. The creation stories, in Genesis 1 and 2, portray the miraculous beginnings of life. Two separate accounts of creation are recorded, and in the second one God creates the heavens and the earth and then causes a mist or flood (Gen. 2:6) to fall upon the earth. Then God forms man from the dust of the ground and breathes into his nostrils the breath of life, and man becomes a living soul. The breath or spirit of God is breathed into men and women, and there is life.

I came across an interesting discovery in preparing a sermon on the meaning of Sabbath. In the fourth commandment, which speaks of God's rest (Exodus 20:11), the word used literally means "to catch one's breath"—which is what God did after creating all that is for six days; then God made that seventh day a holy day.

THE SABBATH AS REFRESHMENT AND RENEWAL

A Sabbath day, a Sabbath experience, is one in which we catch our breath. It is a time when activities cease. Some of us have negative opinions about the Sabbath from our early years. I remember Sunday, our Sabbath day, as a day on which we could do very little. We couldn't play ball, mow grass, shop, or see movies. It was a day to stay home and do as little as possible. I remember, for the most part, the "don'ts," the negatives, the legalism.

In recent years, however, I have come to see the Sabbath in a more positive light, as a time for *refreshment* and *renewal*. Old Testament scholars note that the original Sabbath was a day not of worship but simply of rest. A well-known pastor recounted a conversation with a layman active in his church at the end of a particularly long Sunday of church activity. "I'm sure glad there is only one day of rest per week," the layman observed. "I'd burn out if we had to go through two days of rest like this every seven days."[39]

I don't know when you experience the Sabbath each week. Sunday may not be the day that rest is possible. (For the pastor, it cannot be a day of rest.) The fact remains that we must find times of rest in the midst of activity and work. "The busiest and most active organ in the human body is the heart, which beats 70-75 times a minute, 36 million times a year; and yet those beats always happen on an exertion-rest rhythm. There is exertion, and there is rest. This is the delicate balance of the human heart, and of life."[40]

But there is more here than a principle for living. The scriptures tell us that this is the way God acts, the way that God has created all that is. God's work was followed by a time of refreshment and renewal.

THE SABBATH AS WITNESS

The charge to rest, to refuel, is a sermon that many of us need, whether we hear it from our spouses, our physicians, or a preacher. But there are more reasons to keep the Sabbath. Keeping the Sabbath is also an act of faith, a gesture of trust. The Sabbath is an important part of our heritage as God's people.

In *Finally Comes the Poet*, Walter Brueggemann has noted two crucial motivations for keeping the Sabbath in an age of restlessness: We are called to rest as God rested in the act of creation (Exod. 20:11), and we are to remember, in the midst of Sabbath, "the liberation that permitted new life" (Deut. 5:15). Brueggemann observes that "the two motivations, creation in Exodus 20 and liberation in Deuteronomy 5, hold together the ordered life of God and the just intent of human life. To keep Sabbath is to engage in an activity that holds together, sacramentally, the life of God and the life of the world in liberation."[41]

To observe the Sabbath is to affirm our faith in a God who created the world and holds it together, even as we rest. As we sing in the children's hymn, "He's got the whole world in his hands."

I have a rather brash friend who supervised a seminary intern a couple of summers ago. The student arrived at the beginning of the summer, met the people, and became involved in the work. Toward the end of July my friend, Ralph, informed the student that he was planning to take a week of vacation. A day or two before his departure, the student came forward and expressed some anxiety about Ralph's leaving and her ability to care for the church in his absence. Finally, Ralph said to the student, "This church has been here for 150 years, and you won't be able to kill it in a week!"

"He's got the whole world in his hands," we sing as children. "This earth is the Lord's and all that is in it," the psalmist cries out (Psalm 24:1). As we observe the Sabbath, we express our belief that we belong to this God and to no other. As we observe the Sabbath, we acknowledge that God is the giver and the sustainer of life and that its continuing survival and prosperity does not depend on us. As we observe the Sabbath, we remember that the God who created the earth in six days rested on the seventh.

Someone recently remarked that God's people have never had to work seven days a week. The person concluded that if we labored six days, God would provide for the seventh just as God did with the children of Israel on their journey. Here Brueggemann's connecting of restlessness and greed is particularly perceptive. Sometimes we must miss a Sabbath; even Jesus said that the Sabbath was made for us and not the other way around. But if we find that we are making no room for rest, for the presence of God in our lives, then we may be too busy. And our busyness may mask a lack of trust in the God who provides.

FOCUS

What practical step can you take to implement rest and Sabbath into your own pastoral ministry? How might your theology need to be revised to incorporate the need for Sabbath?

THE SABBATH AS REMINDER OF OUR LIMITATIONS

The Sabbath is a reminder of our human limitations. We cannot do it all. We never could, and we were never expected to do everything. We cannot wait until all the work is done before we accept the gift of Sabbath. The great theologian Karl Barth put it this way:

> If man has created neither heaven and earth nor himself; if he does not owe his existence to himself, but to the will and act of Him who bestowed it on him without his slightest cooperation; if his ability to work is not his attainment and therefore his own property, but a free gift; if his obligation to work is not his invention but God's commission, then he cannot and should not imagine that what is going to become of him, his future and that of his fellow men, lies in his own power.[42]

God has placed limits on us. To everything there is a season, a time and a purpose under heaven. There is a time for work, and as Christians we are called to be faithful, diligent, hardworking, and dependable so that no one can speak ill of our faith. But there is also a time for rest, and as leaders in the community of faith we express this faith in observance of the Sabbath. God created on the first six days; on the seventh day God rested, blessed that day, and made it holy. Let it be the same with us.

FOR REFLECTION

1. Which aspect of the Sabbath is most meaningful to you: Sabbath as re-creation, Sabbath as witness, or Sabbath as reminder of human limitation?
2. When do you observe Sabbath each week?
3. Can you list particular places that are "restful" to you?
4. In what manner was the rest of God on the seventh day "creative"? When are you most creative?
5. What limitations seem most real to you? Can you understand them in light of the biblical concept of Sabbath?

PRAYER

O God,
whose spirit moved over the waters in creation:
move among us, in experiences of rest and Sabbath,
and make of us a new creation,
through Jesus Christ our Lord. Amen.

CHAPTER NINE

Speaking Truth to Power and Other Painful Tasks

2 Samuel 11

┌─────────────── **KEY ISSUES** ───────────────┐

How does the parish pastor exercise the calling to be
a prophet? How do issues of power and money shape
our understandings of vocation and what it means to
be the church? How can we begin to "speak the truth
in love" in matters of stewardship?

└──┘

saiah might not recognize it as a calling, but it's as good as a hot coal
to the Reverend Will B. Dunn, the entrepreneurial preacher of the
award-winning *Kudzu* cartoon strip. "It's a dirty job, but somebody
has to do it," says Dunn as he accedes to a revelation he received while
"taking tea with the Tadsworths in their hot tub." He commits himself
to a "ministry to the fabulously well-to-do." Thus embarked on what is
known in contemporary ecclesiastical lingo as a "specialized ministry,"
Dunn proceeds to encourage his parishioners to beat the bushes in
pursuit of the wealthy and culturally advantaged.

Quite seriously, speaking truth to power is, indeed, a difficult job.
Reinhold Niebuhr acknowledged this fact by his insistence that the
proclamation of the gospel in this world confronted pastors with one
of their greatest problems.

> The practical difficulty of preaching this gospel is that it seems
> least relevant to those people and those generations to whom it is
> most relevant. From the standpoint of the gospel, we must regard
> power, or the wisdom or the security of any man as not being as
> significant as he tries to make himself believe that it is.[43]

49

The relation of the gospel to power and the manner in which the Christian community responds to this "practical difficulty" has been the subject of various attempts to set the discussion within the evangelical counsels of the church: poverty, chastity, and obedience.

Despite their similar titles, *Money, Sex and Power* by Richard Foster, and *Sex, Money and Power* by Philip Turner, are marked by significant differences in both their methods and their conclusions.[44] Foster, author of the popular *Freedom of Simplicity* and *Celebration of Discipline,* calls for a "creative" examination of the relation between money and Christian faith as an alternative to monastic renunciation and Puritan industry.

Foster finds two divergent streams of teaching in the Bible. Texts such as Matthew 6:24 emphasize the dark side and portray money as a potentially dangerous power, while texts such as Matthew 25:14-30 stress its light side and regard material blessings as gifts from a gracious God. Foster offers Christians counsel in "conquering" the dark side of money and encouragement in the practice of graciousness and generosity. Certainly, money can be both a curse and a blessing and can produce both greed and selflessness. Yet in the strength of Foster's position lies his greatest weakness as well. His strategies for dealing with money—listening to biblical teachings about money, examining our inner attitudes toward money, siding with people against money and things, denying favored treatment of the privileged, and offering support and solidarity to the poor—fail to reflect the complexity of any of these actions and to expose the difficulty each presents to the faithful.

In his book Turner offers a more satisfying account of the place of money in the life of the Christian. Primarily concerned "about the ordering of monetary relations within the church," Turner grounds his social ethic upon the provocative assumption that it is the nature of both God and humanity to "give, receive, and return." He says that because presence, reciprocity, giving, receiving, and returning define the deep structure of both divine and human life, then all discussions of economic and sexual relations derive from an immanent understanding of the Trinity, which serves as "the foundation of anthropology and of all social ethics."

The target of Turner's discussion is the church. He is convinced that by ignoring the significance of economic relations within the household of faith the church has erred in two significant ways. First, we have failed to see the potentially powerful influence that the church's own economic witness might have upon society. Second, our evangelistic mission to the world is inevitably hampered by the absence of just and gracious economic relations within the church itself; the truth of the gospel is, after all, to be displayed not only in speech but also by actions. On this point, Ken Callahan's observation that there are often "caste systems" within local churches is particularly relevant.[45]

FOCUS

What is your church's economic witness within the community? Does that witness have any relation to your church's efforts in mission and/or evangelism? Are economic decisions made in consultation with the church's strategic mission?

The relationship between poverty and evangelism, a critical concern for Turner, is also the subject of Segundo Galilea's *The Beatitudes: To Evangelize as Jesus Did.* Galilea's thesis—that identification with the poor is an "essential trait of Christian evangelization"—echoes Turner's insistence upon the interrelatedness of piety and poverty, proclamation and social ethics. Both Turner and Galilea also emphasize the eschatological character of God's reign in economic life, rejecting the more evolutionary model often espoused by liberation theologians, such as Gustav Gutierrez.

Both authors are concerned with the impact of economic practices and attitudes upon the community of faith. Turner poses the metaphor of the body as a guiding image for understanding wealth and poverty: Christians (and in a less explicit way, all members of society) are members of one body, dependent upon one another and with particular gifts to share. Such an image is a challenge to churches, which often mirror cultural divisions of race and class. For Galilea, evangelization must be premised upon a message that is authentically Christian—one that connects spirituality with mission and personal holiness with attentiveness to social justice, and one that calls the rich and the poor to the values of the kingdom.[46]

It is no accident that the beatitudes of Jesus are central to the discussions of both Turner and Galilea. If the authors' reflections on the inevitable tension between the demands of Jesus and the realities of modern life do not result in neatly synthesized conclusions, they are in good company. Reinhold Niebuhr himself struggled with the requirements of the kingdom in *An Interpretation of Christian Ethics*. The varied interpretations of New Testament scholars are due in large part to the difficulty that Jesus' counsels of perfection hold for his followers. Was he being hyperbolic? Are these general principles? Do they presuppose an interim ethic? Is Jesus referring to a future in-breaking of God's reign?

The beatitudes and our reading of them confront us with the very difficulties alluded to by the Reverend Will B. Dunn. Ministry to the comfortable is difficult and "hazardous" precisely because the comfortable are least likely to feel an inclination toward trust in or dependence upon God or any need for "salvation." In this light the first beatitude takes on a new relevance: The poor, who possess the kingdom of God, are blessed.

Yet Niebuhr's insight challenges those who would seek to serve on two counts. To those who have fled the mainline denominational parishes and have dismissed them as hopeless bastions of cultural values and civic religion, Niebuhr's message is pointed: "Part of the task of preaching the gospel is to persuade those people, who think that the gospel is for the weak, that it is for the strong as well; that a strong man is really very weak."[47] To those who are convinced that authentic servanthood in our times can only take place in the Third World or among the urban or rural poor, Niebuhr's voice is a necessary corrective.

But Niebuhr also speaks a dissenting word against those who would become comfortable among the privileged, in those parishes where, in Ernest Campbell's language, "never is heard a discouraging word." No less than other people, many pastors are tempted to be silent in the presence of power and wealth, perhaps because they secretly equate redemption with material success or perhaps because that same desire is present in the pastor. This "revolutionary transmutation of values" bears upon the pastor as well as the businessperson, and the pastor is no less prone to self-deception.

One positive outcome of the recent American Catholic deliberations on economic life has been their willingness to struggle with the ethos that shapes the lives of many of the faithful among varied denominations. If the liberation theologians are correct in insisting that "social location" is crucial in determining one's theological perspective, then one quickly recognizes that what might be appropriate for a base community in Brazil and for a layperson sitting in the pew of a mainline church in middle-class America often differ. The same gospel ought to confront them both, but in opposing ways.

Niebuhr saw the task of the preacher in the midst of affluence in prophetic terms; the message of the modern-day Nathan to David is "Thou are the man." Interestingly, John Langan and John Coleman, both prominent participants in recent Catholic discussions of economic life in North America, have also taken this biblical text (2 Samuel 11, 12) to be paradigmatic for our context. In *An American Strategic Theology,* Coleman has also suggested that North American Christians are called to a "theology of relinquishment" as the means of faithful living and the path to freedom.[48] Turner asserts that as we give of ourselves, we display the inner life of God in our relationships with one another. Renunciation is also, however, a way toward freedom; both Turner and Galilea perceive the Matthean spiritualization of the Beatitudes not as a denial of their material relevance but as a recognition of the interior freedom that comes with evangelical poverty; where one's treasure is, there also is one's heart. Renunciation itself has no intrinsic value apart from its motivation—one is to forsake all things in order to follow Christ.

Turner, Foster, Galilea, and others compel those of us who would live by faith and who would also acknowledge that we are advantaged (by global standards) to evaluate our own attitudes and practices. Perhaps the fictional Rev. Dunn is an accurate depiction of the typical pastor; perhaps we in the mainline denominations have come to our social locations "while taking tea in the Tadworths' hot tub," so to speak. If so, Niebuhr's warning sounds for us all. Between the Scylla of the television preachers and the Charybdis of the liberationists and social activists lies a difficult middle ground, where the gospel is always needed, yet often silent.

FOR REFLECTION

1. Is the gospel difficult to accept by the self-sufficient? Is it difficult to make the gospel relevant to the self-sufficient?
2. How would you define your "social location"? Does it shape your theological perspective? Your attitudes toward money and possessions?
3. Is the gospel fundamentally different for a middle-class parish in Atlanta or Cleveland and a base community in Brazil or Bolivia?

PRAYER

O God,
in our prophecy let us speak your words with our voice;
let us render your judgment with your mercy;
let us measure our power alongside your humility.
Give us grace and courage, to speak and to be silent,
all according to your purposes,
through Jesus Christ our Lord. Amen.

EPILOGUE

A PEOPLE OF GOD'S OWN POSSESSION

Deuteronomy 7

As the people of God, we are to be a "people of God's own possession" (Deuteronomy 7:6, RSV). As members of the Body of Christ, the Apostle Paul reminds us: "You are not your own, . . . you were bought with a price" (1 Corinthians 6:19-20).

I have attempted to reflect on what it might mean to envision the pastoral vocation through the prism of stewardship. My task has been risky, for when many of us hear the word *stewardship,* we perhaps think of next year's annual campaign held in the local church, in which the next year's budget is "raised" and obligations are cemented.

Sadly, most Christians (pastors included) are not aware that the concept of stewardship has a much deeper meaning and a richer history. The image of the Christian as "steward" was a favorite of John Wesley's who preferred it to "debtor" or "servant." Stewardship was quite simply the acknowledgment that "we are indebted to God for all that we have." The steward knows that "he is not at liberty to use what is lodged in his hands as he pleases, but as his master pleases." 49

We are not proprietors; instead, we have been given a conditional trust, to live in accord with the will and the wishes of the master, God. Our own goals, dreams, and ambitions must be reconciled to God's desires for justice and righteousness.

Yet we are also a people caught in a crossfire, to use a metaphor from warfare. On the one side we feel allegiance to cultural, national, and economic forces, which espouse self-determination, freedom of will, and individualism. On the other side we are pulled by the virtues from our heritage of faith—charity, benevolence, justice, concern for the poor, and the good of the community.

Christians have a special vocation in the world, and much of this vocation is "fleshed out" in the ways in which we order the economic lives of our families and parishes. Our vocation or calling is to announce to the world that the claims of God are indeed prior to those of mammon. Rather than seek an abundance of possessions, we are willing to allow ourselves to be in God's possession; this is no more than our commonly shared vow to uphold the Christian community with our "prayers, presence, gifts, and service."

We can consider various strategies for making our way through the crossfire, for living out our vocation. One is to take our place simplistically on one side or the other and to join in the rhetorical fray. Another is to denounce both sides as cynical, without proposing an alternative. Still another is to leave it to one's spouse, say, to be be the charitable and benevolent partner while one goes after the dollar without regard for the other, or to allow the pastor to focus on "spiritual" matters while the laity live in the material world.

Each of these strategies ignores our most basic statement of faith— "Jesus is Lord"—and the challenges that such an affirmation holds for a life guided by this claim. Douglas John Hall has noted that the term *steward* has both positive and negative connotations in scripture. While the steward is identified with the Master, one also tends to forget that she or he is actually a representative and not the owner.[50]

As a people of God's own possession, shaped by the fundamental affirmation that "Jesus is Lord," we learn to discover security in God's guidance and direction. Although materialism lures us with the seeming security of material goods, the biblical provision is for *daily bread*. The drama of God's provision is told in the story of the wandering people of Israel, who were promised daily bread, holy manna, but no more than a day's provision. The story, rich in detail and implication, tells of a people utterly dependent on God, failing at times, but turning again and again to God's leading.

We live in a dangerous, unpredictable world. Uncertainties are a given. Nevertheless, the biblical truth is simple, yet not simplistic: God is our security; in God's service is "perfect freedom"; a surrender to the divine will is the beginning of new possibilities of grace.

In the end, the people of God's own possession are those who know that the struggle of faithfulness in economic practices is played out in the presence of God's justice and forgiveness. God demands that we act as stewards of God's gifts, that we serve God and God alone. Yet our labors, our plans, and our programs still fall short of the divine economy. The summary of faith extends also to economic life and to the pastor who would also be a steward: We are saved by grace, yet we are also "created in Christ Jesus for good works" (Eph. 2:8, 10).

ENDNOTES

1. William Barclay, *Ethics in a Permissive Society* (New York: Harper and Row, 1971), p. 162.

2. John Wesley's *Forty-Four Sermons* (London: Epworth Press, 1977), p. 577.

3. Karl Barth, *Deliverance to the Captives* (New York: Harper and Row, 1961), p. 40.

4. Stanley Hauerwas, *The Peaceable Kingdom* (Notre Dame: University of Notre Dame Press, 1983), p. 27.

5. To compare the accounts, see Mark 10:17-31; Matthew 19:16-30; Luke 18:18-30. For a concise summary of varying interpretations of this memorable passage see Lamar Williamson, *Mark: Interpretation: A Bible Commentary for Teaching and Preaching* (Atlanta: John Knox Press, 1983), pp. 187-188).

6. Ernest Campbell, Lectures at Wake Forest University Pastor's School, July 1986.

7. Geoffrey Wainwright, *Doxology* (New York: Oxford University Press, 1980), p. 422.

8. Reinhold Niebuhr, *Justice and Mercy* (New York: Harper and Row, 1974), pp. 64, 69.

9. Alan Jones, *Exploring Spiritual Direction* (New York: Seabury, 1980), p. 30.

10. Kennon Callahan suggests that the discovery of meaning and purpose in life arises out of participation in mission toward the hopes and hurts of others. See *Twelve Keys to an Effective Church* (San Francisco: Harper and Row, 1983).

11. St. Augustine, *Confessions* (Philadelphia: Westminster, 1955), 1/1.

12. Campbell, *Where Cross the Crowded Ways* (New York: Association Press, 1973), p. 30.

13. Philip Turner, *Sex, Money and Power* (Cambridge, Mass.: Cowley Press, 1985).

14. John Killinger, "Hold and Let Go," *alive now!* May/June, 1981, pp. 8-9. Used by permission.

15. Anthony Bloom, *Beginning to Pray* (New York: Paulist Press, 1970), p. 41.

16. Elaine Pagels, *Adam, Eve and the Serpent* (New York: Random House, 1988).

17. Thomas Aquinas, *Summa Theologica*, Volume Two, Part One (New York, 1955).

18. David Burrell, *Aquinas: God and Action* (Notre Dame: University of Notre Dame Press, 1979), pp. 165-166.

19. Fred Craddock, *Preaching* (Nashville: Abingdon Press, 1985), p. 69.

20. Ralph C. Wood, "Charge to the Quail Hollow Presbyterian Church at the Installation of Timothy Stuart Hood as Its Pastor, Minister and Preacher," Charlotte, North Carolina, March 8, 1987.

21. Diana and David Garland, *Beyond Companionship: Christians in Marriage* (Philadelphia: Westminster, 1986), p. 28.

22. Lisa Sowle Cahill, *Between the Sexes* (New York: Paulist and Fortress Presses, 1985), p. 56.

23. Ibid., p. 1.

24. Ibid., pp. 11, 150-152.

25. Ray Anderson and Dennis Guernsey, *On Being Family* (Grand Rapids: Eerdmans, 1985), p. 26.

26. *The United Methodist Hymnal* (Nashville: United Methodist Publishing House, 1989), p. 866.

27. See Karl Barth, *Church Dogmatics,* IV, III (Edinburgh: T and T Clark, 1975) and Dietrich Bonhoeffer, *Letters and Papers from Prison* (New York: MacMillan, 1967).

28. Quoted in Williams and Hauck, *The Judeao-Christian Vision and the Modern Corporation,* 1982, p. 318.

29. *The United Methodist Hymnal,* p. 724.

30. Donald Jones, ed., *Business, Religion and Ethics: Inquiry and Encounter* (Cambridge, Mass.: Oelgeschlager, Gunn and Hain, 1982), pp. 219-220.

31. Turner, p. 75.

32. John C. Raines and Donna C. Day-Lower, *Modern Work and Human Meaning* (Philadelphia: Westminster, 1986), pp. 15-16, 17.

33. Gilbert Meilaender, *Friendship* (Notre Dame: University of Notre Dame Press, 1981), p. 97.

34. Studs Terkel, *Working* (New York: Avon, 1972), p. xiii.

35. David Halberstam, *The Reckoning* (New York: William Morrow, 1986), p. 616.

36. See J. Philip Wogaman, *Economics and Ethics:* A CHRISTIAN INQUIRY (Philadelphia: Fortress Press, 1986).

37. John Haughey, S. J., *The Holy Use of Money* (New York: Doubleday, 1985), p. 54.

38. Wogaman, esp. Chapters 3 and 10.

39. Gordon MacDonald, *Ordering Your Private World* (Nashville: Thomas Nelson, 1984), p. 184.

40. Wayne Oates, *Your Right to Rest* (Philadelphia: Westminster, 1984), p. 29.

41. Walter Brueggemann, *Finally Comes the Poet* (Minneapolis: Fortress, 1989), p. 92.

42. Barth, *Church Dogmatics,* III, IV, p. 54.

43. Niebuhr, p. 132.

44. See Richard Foster, *Money, Sex and Power* (San Francisco: Harper and Row, 1985), and Philip Turner, *Sex, Money and Power* (Cambridge, Mass.: Cowley Press, 1985).

45. See Callahan, *Effective Church Leadership* (San Francisco: Harper and Row, 1990).

46. See Turner; Segundo Galilea, *The Beatitudes* (Maryknoll, NY: Orbis Press, 1984).

47. Niebuhr, p. 133.

48. John Coleman, *An American Strategic Theology* (New York: Paulist, 1982).

49. Albert Outler, ed., *John Wesley* (New York: Oxford Press, 1964), pp. 282-283.

50. Douglas John Hall, *The Steward: A Biblical Symbol Come of Age* (New York: Friendship Press, 1982), p. 19.